DOGS

DOGS

Don Harper

PARRAGON

Acknowledgements

Animals Unlimited page 21; **Simon Bannister/Animal Photography** page 61; **Bruce Coleman Ltd/Thomas Buchholz** page 17; /**Jane Burton** pages 25, 62, 66, 68, 73, 78 left; /**John Cancalosi** page 71; /**Erich Crichton** page 31; /**Stephen J. Krasemann** page 8; /**Eckart Pott** pages 22, 75; /**Fritz Prenzel** page 35; /**Hans Reinhard** pages 6, 9, 13, 26, 28, 29, 32, 37, 38, 40, 41, 42, 47, 49, 50–51, 52, 55, 56, 57, 58, 60, 63, 77; /**Kim Taylor** page 78 right; /**K. Wothe** page 45; /**Gunther Ziesler** page 74; **Sally Anne Thompson/Animal Photography** jacket, pages 10, 18, 65, 69; **R. Wilbie/Animal Photography** pages 14–15.

First published in Great Britain in 1994 by
Parragon Book Service Ltd
Units 13-17, Avonbridge Trading Estate
Atlantic Road, Avonmouth
Bristol BS11 9QD

Publishing Manager: Sally Harper
Editor: Anne Crane
Design: Robert Mathias/Helen Mathias

ISBN 1 85813 866 3

Printed in Italy

Contents

CHAPTER ONE

Early Days

FACING PAGE: Many breeds of dog, such as border collies and other sheepdogs, exist because of human needs for working animals.

It is an amazing fact that all of today's 350 or so breeds of domestic dog, from the tiny Chihuahua to the huge Irish wolfhound, are descended from the grey wolf *(Canis lupus)*. The origins of this tremendous diversity lie in the wolf's past. It used to be the most widely distributed wild animal in the northern hemisphere. Grey wolves were encountered throughout North America, as well as in Europe and Asia, where their range extended southwards across the entire Arabian peninsula.

Individual populations of the grey wolf differed noticeably in size through this huge area. This variation is a characteristic which has since become more apparent in domestic dogs today. The biggest of all grey wolves still occur in Alaska, where their strength is required to overcome large and potentially dangerous quarry such as moose. They can stand 90 cm (35 in) tall, whereas in contrast, the now-extinct Shamanu grey wolf, which occurred in Japan, measured just 39 cm (14 in) at the shoulder.

Zoologists have identified some 30 distinct past and present forms of the grey wolf, based not only on variations in size, but also in their coloration. While some populations are decidedly greyish, the striking Newfoundland white wolf (which became extinct around 1911), for example, was pure white in coloration, with just a slight tinge of ivory evident on its head and limbs. Grey wolves from other areas could vary from shades of yellow through brown to black, and such diver-

ABOVE: *The grey wolf is the ancestor of the hundreds of dog breeds that we know today.*

sity helps to explain the wide range of colours and markings seen in domestic dogs today.

It is believed that perhaps four distinct forms of the grey wolf contributed to the ancestry of the domestic dog, with domestication occurring in several parts of the world, probably at different times. Almost certainly, the bond between humans and canids existed long before this process began in earnest, however, and it could have been forged for the first time perhaps 40,000 years ago.

Wolves and people were already widely dispersed across the northern hemisphere at this stage, and both were predatory species. Each group relied upon co-operative hunting to overcome the huge herbivores such as the mammoths which were a dominant feature of the Ice Age fauna.

Abandoned or orphaned wolf cubs may have been cared for by people at this stage, in the same way that jungle tribespeople often rear parrots and other wild animals in their villages today. The young wolf could in turn have repaid this kindness by alerting the people to danger, particularly after dark, when its keener sense of hearing would have proved to be invaluable. A tame wolf may also have been of some assistance when hunting, indicating the presence of likely quarry, and even helping to slow it down during the chase, enabling the hunters to inflict a fatal blow.

If food was short, however, there was also the possibility of eating the wolf. Although this is now an abhorrent idea to Western sensibilities, canids have remained a popular source of food in the East, right up to the present.

The start of domestication

Archaeological evidence suggests that the domestication process did not start until the end of the Pleistocene era, about 12,000 years ago. At this stage, the climate began to change, becoming less harsh. The human population started to live a more settled existence, with farming becoming more widespread.

It seems that the present-day area of the Middle East was an early focus for a closer relationship between people and canids. In northern Israel, for example, a skeleton of a dog was discovered buried in the same grave as that of a person whose arm had been placed around the

dog, indicating a bond between them. Additional evidence to support this theory has come from Jericho and Iraq, where the remains of early domestic dogs have been found.

The dogs of this era were already diverging from the native wolf population in the region. They were not as tall. Their teeth were also smaller, and this has since become even more noticeable in domestic dogs.

The first evidence of distinctive divisions within the dog population itself comes from North America. Here, in the vicinity of the Beaverhead Mountains of eastern central Idaho, the remains of two different types of dog have been unearthed, dating back about 9,000 years. The larger form, equivalent in size to a modern-day retriever, was clearly of different appearance to the smaller, beagle-like dog.

Almost inevitably, selection pressures were brought to bear on dogs from these early days. It would have been desirable, for example, to have individual dogs

LEFT: *Evidence of the bond between humans and dogs shows that the relationship reaches back about 12,000 years.*

which responded well to humans, and these would have been favoured for breeding purposes. Size was also likely to have proved significant, especially since small dogs eat less than their larger relatives. They are also easier to control in most cases, which could have proved advantageous.

A unique breeding project

An interesting insight into the way in which the wolf's temperament and behaviour would have been altered in those early days has been provided by a recent breeding experiment which began in the Netherlands. Here in the 1930s, a dog breeder called Leendert Saarloos decided to cross grey wolves and dogs, believing that the domestic dog had been weakened through many generations of selective breeding. Saarloos chose the German shepherd dog because of its similarity to the grey wolf.

His initial plans were rather compromised by the death of the wolf however, as the result of a viral infection which may have been acquired from the dog. But he persevered, obtained another wolf, and ultimately hybrid puppies were

FACING PAGE: The Saarloos-wolfhond is the result of deliberately breeding wolves with German shepherd dogs.

born. They proved far less tractable than young pure-bred dogs, and were also more nervous by nature.

For the rest of his life, Saarloos continued this experimental breeding programme, diluting the wolf genes by using German shepherd dogs and so refining the temperament of the emerging breed. When he finally died in 1969, his dream of attaining official recognition for these dogs had not been achieved. There was then a real risk that his endeavours would never be acknowledged, but supporters rallied round, and the breed was recognized by the Dutch Kennel Club six years later, under the name of the Saarloos-wolfhond.

Ownership today is still confined to a dedicated band of breeders, and although more than half a century has passed since Saarloos began his breeding programme, these dogs still display strong lupine (wolf-like) behavioural traits. Similar responses would doubtless have been evident during the early days of the domestication process.

Saarlooswolfhonds retain strong pack instincts, and a distinct social structure is apparent within each group. They will not thrive if kept in isolation, needing to

11

live in pairs at the very least, or preferably larger groups, to give them a greater sense of security.

The Saarlooswolfhond is not an easy breed to train, especially when compared with the German shepherd dog, which is very responsive. In terms of their pattern of vocalization, these hybrid dogs may also appear more closely allied to wolves than domestic dogs.

Barking is very much a feature which has been emphasized through domestication. Wolves in fact are relatively quiet, although they are likely to howl, particularly after a kill. But they will only bark in quiet tones close to their den, to indicate alarm. Similarly, Saarlooswolfhonds do not tend to bark, using their body language instead to indicate the presence of strangers in their vicinity.

Domestication underway

Very few entire skeletons of early dogs have been unearthed, so it can be difficult to gain a clear impression of their overall appearance. They were almost certainly used for hunting purposes though, and so some may not have been dissimilar in appearance to greyhounds, with pace and keen eyesight being vital hunting characteristics. For example, remains unearthed at Vlasac in Romania are of dogs alone, with no traces of other domestic animals. This tends to indicate that they were being used as hunting companions at this stage, and possibly also as a direct source of meat.

Some of today's characteristic physical changes had occurred quite early during the domestication process, such as a shortening of the facial area in some dogs. This feature has subsequently been developed in modern times in breeds such as the bulldog with its massive, short, square head.

Almost certainly, however, our record of the early domestication of the dog is very incomplete. Undoubtedly, the larger, more northern races of the grey wolf would also have played a significant part, but actual evidence for this is distinctly limited. In North America, these would probably have been the ancestors of today's Eskimo breeds, while in northeastern Asia, the wolves here would have contributed to the mastiff line of domestic dogs.

The concept of actual breeds is a very recent phenomenon. It was triggered by the rising interest in exhibiting dogs in Victorian England. Nevertheless, it is possible to trace the lineage of some contemporary groups, such as mastiffs, back thousands of years, to portrayals of such dogs on tombs.

The development of dogs for specific purposes had begun by Roman times. They had dogs to fulfil a variety of tasks, and were keen to add to their own stock, as they conquered foreign lands.

In Britain, it is believed that the Celts introduced large mastiff-type dogs soon after their arrival in 400 BC. Although relatively slow, these large dogs did not lack courage, being used for hunting wild boar, which could be a dangerous adversary. Julius Caesar, who led the Roman invasions of Britain in 55 and 54 BC, showed how these mastiffs could become highly rated combatants in the amphitheatres of Rome, where blood flowed freely. Portrayals of such dogs can be found on contemporary mosaics of the Roman period. These dogs were said to be capa-

RIGHT: *Pack hounds such as basset hounds were originally bred to emphasize their hunting abilities.*

13

ble of breaking a bull's neck with a single blow.

But it appears that there were also early hounds being kept in Romano-Britain, which were valued not for their strength, but rather for their sporting prowess. Known to the Romans as vertragus, the origins of these dogs are obscure, but there is little doubt that they were similar to greyhounds in appearance. They had the pace to outrun hares, and were a combination of lemon and white in colour. Some people believe that the vertragus was descended from the saluki, an ancient coursing breed from the Middle East. The ancestors of these dogs could have been brought to Britain by Phoenician traders, who plied around the shores of the Mediterranean and Europe.

The demand for dogs from Britain reached such a level before the end of the Roman Empire that a special official, called the *procurator cynegii*, was based at Winchester to oversee collection and shipment of such dogs back to Rome. Unfortunately, relatively little evidence of their existence, in the form of skeletons, remains today. Although it may seem strange with hindsight, this is partly because early archaeologists often had no

interest in this type of find, and such bones were readily discarded. Complete skeletons are exceedingly rare, with only two being recorded from this era.

A study of just over 1,100 partial specimens has revealed that dogs at this stage ranged in height from 71 cm (28 in) down to just 23 cm (9 in), which indicates that already dogs were probably being kept as companions. Unfortunately, although it is possible to build up an idea of a dog's facial characteristics from its skeleton, there is no means of assessing other aspects of its physical appearance, such as its coat length, coloration or even the shape of its ears. But a fascinating glimpse of small dogs from this era has been found in what is now the state of Arizona. Here, the remains of mummified black-and-white long-haired dogs of terrier type have been discovered.

Contemporary descriptions and portrayals can be helpful in piecing together the likely appearance of European dogs during the Roman period. Those that were bred for specific purposes were

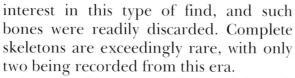

LEFT: *Feral dogs can be 're-domesticated': the Canaan dog was developed in Israel from the indigenous pariah dogs.*

paired together, and so tended to develop a similar appearance. There was the agassaeus, for example, a small breed of hound which was lean and characterized by its shaggy coat. It was well known for its tracking skills, possessing a keen sense of smell, in contrast to the vertragus which hunted by sight.

There is also more obvious evidence of the functions of dogs at this early stage in history. Mosaics bearing images of prick-eared dogs, with longish, upright tails, have been unearthed in various Roman homes. They carry the inscription *Cave canem*, meaning 'Beware of the dog', indicating that dogs were being used to protect private property.

The dog's fortunes decline

The break up of the Roman Empire and the start of the Dark Age saw dramatic changes, which extended to the dog population as well. In Britain, the small toy breeds seemed to have disappeared, or at least became much scarcer, while hunting patterns changed.

During the Roman period, dogs and people had worked together to catch game. Now hunting became a faster and potentially more dangerous pastime. The huntsmen themselves took to horses, and so began the tradition of riding with the hounds, which has continued now for nearly two millennia. The quarry in those days was potentially more fearsome however, with wild boar being highly prized. Perhaps not surprisingly, only the king and his companions were permitted to hunt deer in the royal forests, which were a much safer quarry.

Elaborate laws were devised to outlaw illegal hunting by ordinary people, with only the wealthy being allowed to own suitable dogs. Hounds kept by commoners were deliberately handicapped, by having tendons cut or claws removed, to deter their use for hunting in the royal forests. An exception was made for the purpose of hunting wolves, which were still numerous in Britain at this time. But contemporary accounts suggest they were often elusive quarry, still able to outpace their domesticated relatives largely by their superior stamina. Such was the problem posed by wolves that criminals were sentenced to hunt them, as an alternative to other punishments.

There seem to be no records of wolfhounds at this stage in history. In fact, there appear to have been only two distinctive types of dog in England then, with the number having declined since the end of the Roman era.

The Middle Ages saw the continued use of the dog in combat, and as a fierce protector at home. Located in Warwick Castle, under Guy's Tower, is a large stone opening, leading to a chamber. Here, constantly alert to the threat of danger, were housed the canine guardians of that era, whose modern descendants still exist.

The most feared, according to contemporary accounts, was the massive Irish hound, which was taller than any other dog, being equivalent in size to a large calf. It would have towered above today's Irish wolfhound, being more than 1.2 m (4 ft) in height at the shoulder, with a skull which measured at least 43 cm (17 in) in length. Its appearance suggested that it was the result of a cross between greyhound and mastiff stock. The majority were apparently a sandy shade in terms of coloration. Few argued with these fearsome giants, which possessed both immense strength and loyal, protective instincts.

The legend of Gelert has become well

known, and is typical of the way in which these Irish hounds would defend family members to the death. Gelert, an Irish hound, was left guarding a baby while his owner Llewelyn went out hunting. On his return, Llewelyn was horrified to be greeted by the sight of an overturned cot, stained with blood, and the presence of blood on Gelert's face and body. He killed the dog instantly with his sword, at which point, he heard the baby cry out from under the cot. On venturing further into the room, Llewelyn found the baby unharmed, and the body of a wolf nearby. Horrified by his actions, Llewelyn was reputed to have buried the dog close to his lodge at the village of Beddgelert in Wales, marking the spot with a cairn of stones.

This version of the story was promulgated by David Pritchard, as a means of boosting trade when he took over the Royal Goat Inn there. He even buried a dog beneath the cairn, with the con-

RIGHT: *Dogs have long proved themselves to be deeply loyal – even to the point of sacrificing their own lives.*

nivance of the parish clerk, to verify the story, although the skeletal remains later excavated there were far too small to be those of an Irish hound.

Mastiffs could be equally loyal to their owners, even defending them in the confusion and noise of the battlefield. Many of these dogs were equipped with special spiked collars, which helped to protect the vulnerable area of their throats from attack. They were sometimes specially bred for combat, being pitted against an armed opponent during their training.

The most famous incident involving a mastiff took place at the battle of Agincourt in 1415. An English knight called Sir Piers Leigh fell badly wounded, but his mastiff bravely guarded the fallen knight until help arrived. They then returned to Cheshire, where Sir Piers died soon afterwards as a result of his injuries. Nevertheless, his famous Lyme Hall strain of mastiffs continued to be bred for centuries, with direct descendants of this particular bitch appearing at the early Victorian dog shows. The influence of the Lyme Hall bloodline is still apparent in the breed, more than 500 years after that fateful day.

Other dogs from this era fared less

well, however, and are now extinct. These include the fearsome alaunt, which was apparently not only kept in Britain but quite widely in Europe as well. The breed may have originated in Spain, where it was kept for animal-baiting purposes. It was generally considered to be of rather limited intelligence, compared with other breeds. Several local variants of the alaunt were described by contemporary writers. There is no doubting the ferocity of these dogs, which were quite capable of killing their owners.

Some alaunts were kept by butchers to drive cattle to town, and to round up any escapees. This may have led to their involvement in bull-baiting spectacles. Their main function was probably in battle, however, where they often proved deadly combatants. Henry VIII took 400 alaunts on his campaign against the French, but the advent of firearms soon spelt the end of such war dogs, and the alaunt disappeared. Its image still survives in heraldic art, with a pair of alaunts being portrayed holding the shield of Lord Dacre of Hurstmonceaux.

Strength and ferocity by humans and dogs on the battlefield may have won the day in these savage conflicts, but then the

victor needed to pursue his fleeing opponents and capture them. Here the keen scenting abilities of the dog could prove of great assistance. The Talbot hound was more than equal to this task. In one famous incident, after being tracked over a considerable distance by his own hound, which had been captured, Robert the Bruce of Scotland overcame his English pursuers by killing them.

Talbot hounds were also used to track cattle rustlers and sheep stealers. Their tradition is maintained today by the bloodhound, which was a name originally given to the Talbot hound. The precise relationship between these breeds is unclear. It seems probable that the bloodhound, at least in part, is descended from the Talbot hound, tracking its quarry with similar determination. Bloodhounds have been known to follow trails which were made days before.

The rise of spaniels

The more settled life-style which started to develop during the late Middle Ages saw the increasing use of dogs for hunting purposes, with newcomers such as spaniels emerging on to the scene. Their

FACING PAGE: It is hard to believe that Great Danes and Yorkshire terriers have the same genetic roots.

name originates from the word espagnol, meaning Spanish, reflecting their country of origin.

These early spaniels were used to hunt birds, either driving them up from undergrowth, so falcons could seize them, or simply indicating their presence, so enabling their capture by nets. They would also seize diving waterfowl, being prepared to enter water readily.

Clear divisions also started to become well established among the hounds of this era, with particular coloration or markings serving to signify specific types. There was the black-and-white patterning of the St Hubert and the tawny-red coat of the Breton hound. But these were relatively slow, and largely used in contrived hunts in the royal deer parks, rather than across open country.

Domestication across the globe

Not surprisingly, relatively few breeds arose at an early stage outside the natural distribution of the grey wolf. South America, for example, possesses little evidence of early dogs. But in Peru, the breed now known as the Peruvian Inca orchid was discovered by the Spanish invaders of the fifteenth century, living in the homes of the wealthy. These dogs are traditionally hairless, apart from traces of hair most noticeable on their head and tail. This breed, although scarce, still survives today, along with its close relative, the Inca hairless dog, which is dark in coloration.

It seems likely that the ancestors of these breeds were taken south at some relatively early stage in history. The hairless gene may then have become apparent as the result of in-breeding over successive generations. Interestingly, dogs with hair are sometimes produced in litters from hairless parents, and are today described by dog fanciers as powder puffs.

Similar hairless dogs originated in China, where it is clear that dogs were domesticated centuries ago, certainly by 550 BC. A number of today's breeds, such as the Pekingese, originated from this part of the world, while the hairless Chinese crested dog is the best known of this type of breed.

Native breeds of dog are scarce in Africa. As in South America, no grey wolves occurred there, and the majority of breeds originating from this continent,

FACING PAGE: *The Chinese crested dog is the best known of the hairless breeds.*

20

such as the Rhodesian ridgeback, are of recent origin, being developed by European settlers. Even so, there are exceptions, such as the azawakh, a sight hound bred by the nomadic Tuareg people of the southern Sahara. It is becoming better known in Europe, after centuries of isolation. Its origins may lie with the hounds of ancient Egypt.

There is also the basenji, which is more widely kept in the Western world. Originating from Zaire, its roots are obscure. It is sometimes described as the barkless dog, although it is capable of growling. This hunting breed may be descended from dogs which were kept in Egypt about 4,000 years ago.

In Africa and elsewhere, there are also pariah dogs – these are feral dogs, which have reverted to living wild, after being domesticated. They tend to scavenge close to human settlements. It has subsequently proved possible to domesticate such dogs again, as shown recently by the case of the Canaan dog. This breed was developed in Israel, as a result of a breeding programme that began in 1935, from the indigenous pariah dogs which had lived in this region for thousands of years.

CHAPTER TWO

Changing Relationships

FACING PAGE: *In the sixteenth century, spaniels were used to catch waterfowl and other birds.*

The Renaissance saw a reappraisal of the relationship between dogs and people, particularly in the royal courts of Europe. Here, small dogs became very popular as ladies' companions. Indeed, Henry VIII took the unusual step of prohibiting all dogs from being kept at Court, apart from small pet spaniels.

Mastiffs continued to enjoy favour through this era, as the popularity of bear and bull-baiting grew under royal patronage. The first book ever published entirely on dogs appeared during this time, indicating their growing popularity. It was written by Dr John Caius, who became the court physician, in response to a request from a famous Swiss naturalist, Conrad Gesner for information on the types of dog being kept in Britain. Pub-

lished in 1570, under the Latin title of *De Canibus Britannicis*, this work also represented the first attempt to classify dogs into distinctive categories.

Caius's writings give a fascinating insight into the range of dogs that were being kept during the late sixteenth century. He refers to six basic divisions. There were the so-called thoroughbred dogs, including harriers and terriers, which were already being used to drive foxes and badgers from their underground lairs, so that they could be chased by hounds. Then there were the hunting dogs, which included greyhounds and limers. Greyhounds were pitted against foxes, but more often deer, while limers, which hunted by scent, were probably the ancestors of today's bloodhounds.

Smaller greyhound-type dogs, called tumblers, chased rabbits, but they appear to have left no descendants.

Working dogs were clearly important at this stage, with sheepdogs being recognized, along with the mastiff. Both spaniels and water spaniels, as well as setters, featured in Caius's Hawking and Fowling group. These dogs were used to catch waterfowl and other birds, sometimes with the assistance of hawks.

Clearly, there was already a significant movement of dogs taking place between different European countries at this time, with Dr Caius describing a new spaniel, which was black and white in colour, and had recently been introduced from France. But he evidently disliked the Icelandic dogs which were also being brought to Britain then, noting that they were not only bad-tempered, but displayed a strange propensity for eating candles. He did not approve of so-called comforter dogs either, which were the fashionable ladies' pets of the period. According to Caius, their origins lay in Malta, with the smallest individuals being the most highly prized. Such dogs were fed at the table and even shared the beds of their owners.

The final group of dogs which Caius identified were simply known as Degenerates. They appear to have fulfilled a variety of tasks, and probably lacked the relative standardization in appearance which was becoming evident as the result of selective breeding of members of the other groups. There was the so-called wappe, kept to guard the home, which barked loudly at the approach of visitors. Other dogs, called turnspits, were trained to turn the roasting meat above the fire in the kitchen, on a type of treadmill. There were also dancing dogs, which provided popular entertainment. They danced to music, and performed tricks in front of an audience.

A period out of favour

The religious changes which swept the country during the sixteenth century left their mark on the canine as well as the human population. Dogs, especially sheepdogs, had long attended church, with special benches being provided for the dogs at the rear of the building, where they could sit alongside their owners. But on Christmas Day 1638, an unfortunate and highly publicized inci-

FACING PAGE: *Foxhounds were bred to increase their speed and endurance, and became able to outrun stage coaches.*

dent occurred in Tadlow. A dog ran up to the altar and seized the bread being prepared for the Communion service, running off with it. This was clearly not an isolated incident: previously, the Bishop of Norwich had instructed churches to place rails to prevent dogs from gaining access to the altar area.

It was not long before owners were being fined for bringing dogs to church, and ecclesiastical dog whippers were instructed to drive any dogs out of the church. They were equipped with spiked tongs, to seize dogs which had retreated under benches.

For the first time, there was also growing awareness of the potential health threat to people resulting from dogs, in terms of the spread of plague, although the exact mechanism was not understood. In reality, fleas from rats could spread to dogs, carrying the deadly plague bacteria into domestic surroundings with them, and then infecting people. At the height of the Great Plague of London in 1666, when the official dog killers were on the streets, more than 40,000 dogs were destroyed. The dog killers were equipped with a special uniform, made out of dog skins.

After the overthrow of the monarchy, hunting went into decline, as did hounds, although Oliver Cromwell hunted hares, and kept a greyhound, strangely known as Coffin-nail. Other activities, such as bear-baiting, were outlawed, although the bulldog survived this period.

Canine companions

The Restoration marked a significant change in attitudes towards dogs, with Charles II himself falling under the spell of small spaniels. His love of this breed first started when he was visited by Henrietta of Orleans, who owned a black-and-white toy spaniel, which she brought with her from France. Such spaniels were soon a common sight at Charles's court, and ultimately, the breed was named after him.

Small dogs were also popular among the House of Orange, notably the pug, which is though to have been introduced to Europe from China. The alert barking of one of these lap dogs had saved the Prince of Orange from assassination, and so became indelibly linked with the Dutch royal family. Not surprisingly, therefore, William brought pugs to England when

he ascended the throne with Mary at the end of the seventeenth century.

The sheer pleasure of companionship provided by dogs became more evident during the subsequent century. New breeds from overseas continued to be introduced, such as the small, rather delicate, Italian greyhound. These small dogs were equipped with warm clothing to protect them from the cold.

Awareness that selective breeding could dramatically affect a dog's performance was growing, and demonstrated in a most dramatic way by Hugo Meynell. He lived at Quornden Hall in Leicestershire, which was to become the headquarters of one of the most famous hunts of all time, known as the Quorn.

Foxhounds of the early 1700s were still lacking the necessary qualities to outrun their quarry effectively. As a result, Meynell decided to embark on a specific breeding plan, to improve both their pace and endurance. Soon, his hounds were capable of outrunning stage coaches, which could then reach speeds of 21 km/hour (13 mph).

The origins of the modern foxhound date from this era, as do many of today's terrier breeds, the vast majority of which

FACING PAGE: *From having a place in every part of social life, dogs fell out of favour, and were blamed for spreading disease.*

were bred in Britain. Their contribution to the fox-hunting scene called for considerable bravery, driving the larger fox out of its burrow.

As transportation improved, so dogs played their part in safeguarding their owners. Distinctive breeds used for this purpose were the Great Dane, which was originally brought to Britain from Denmark, and the Dalmatian. Contemporary records suggest that the Great Dane, which occurred in three colour forms at that time, was considered to be the more desirable of the pair. It protected the contents of the carriage from thieves, and helped to prevent the horses from being disturbed. The Dalmatian, which tended to trot alongside the carriage as a deterrent to highwaymen, was somewhat smaller.

Various other types of dog were being brought to Europe from further afield, such as early labradors from Newfoundland, not to mention the Newfoundland itself. Both these dogs were sailors' companions, and well adapted to long and

LEFT: *In the late 1700s, some dogs were seen more as companions than as workers, and were brought into the home.*

sometimes perilous sea voyages across the North Atlantic. Certain companion dogs such as the Pomeranian also extended their following beyond their country of origin at this stage. Dogs of very similar type had been among the first small dogs to be kept as pets in Europe, back in the Roman era.

Now as the nineteenth century approached, so the emphasis was to switch firmly away from dogs serving people to a new relationship.

The rise of the dog show

Dog shows, in an informal sense, had begun as early as 1775, with Masters of Hounds showing their packs in the summer, before the start of the hunting season. Charles Aistrop, landlord of the Elephant and Castle public house in Westminster, had learnt at first hand the risks posed by bear-baiting, when a bear killed his wife. Searching for alternative popular entertainment, he was one of the

RIGHT: *Dalmatians were used to guard carriages; there was a danger that they would be hurt by the carriage wheels or kicked by the horses.*

29

first to organize a dog show on more formal lines at his pub during 1834, and he offered a silver cream jug as a prize.

These events proved successful, and Aistrop continued them when he moved to another pub, called the Eight Bells. Contemporary accounts reveal that a range of small breeds could be seen here at the regular Tuesday-night events, including relative rarities such as the Isle of Skye terrier.

Cruft's Great Dog Show

In the late 1860s, Aistrop relinquished his established post in the Toy Spaniel Club, and was succeeded by a man called Charles Cruft. Cruft pioneered the notion of prepared dog food, selling this new idea to the kennels of the aristocracy. He appreciated the value of good promotion, as his rivals started to sell their own brands.

Having been involved in running the dog show which formed part of the Paris Exhibition in 1878, Cruft decided to launch a terrier show in London, drawing on the support and encouragement of wealthy patrons such as the Duchess of Newcastle.

The first event took place at the Royal Aquarium in 1886. The growth of the rail network from London, and rising prosperity, coupled with the innate curiosity of the Victorians, meant that many people were willing to travel to these shows.

In 1891, building on his earlier success, he launched it under the banner of 'Cruft's Great Dog Show', and took an advertisement on the front page of *The Times* newspaper, promising visitors the chance to see the largest and finest group of dogs ever brought together, from all parts of the world, with every breed represented.

This was, of course, not strictly true, but the publicity worked, and Cruft's crowning achievement was to persuade Queen Victoria, herself a great dog lover, to enter some of her Pomeranians.

His show has since become a much-loved national institution, now seen on television around the world. At a time when the traditional skills of working dogs were becoming less valued, so Cruft encouraged the adoption of dogs as household pets. Many of today's popular breeds were introduced to the public at Cruft's shows.

FACING PAGE: *Miniature poodles being judged at Cruft's, where many popular breeds have been introduced to the public.*

Types of Dog

There are now more than 350 different breeds of dog in the world, although some are very rare, and are at risk of becoming extinct. The Tahltan bear dog of Canada, for example, is now doomed, with no male dogs surviving. It was used by the Tahltan Indian tribe to assist them in hunting bears.

In some cases, however, it has proved possible to rescue breeds from near extinction. This happened recently with the shar-pei, an ancient Chinese breed, characterized by its unusual bluish tongue and heavily wrinkled skin. These dogs were believed to have already vanished in China, with only a few surviving in Hong Kong, when Matgo Law wrote an article about their plight, asking for assistance to save them, in a North Ameri-can dog magazine. A number of breeders wrote offering support, and soon the breed was established in the United States. Others reached Europe, and proved very popular. Plucked back from the point of extinction in barely a decade, the shar-pei is now widely kept, and its future seems secure.

Yet it is not only a matter of preserving established breeds. New breeds are also being developed by breeders in response to particular requirements. One of the most recent additions to the list of the world's dogs is the kyi leo, a diminutive breed measuring up to 30 cm (12 in) high at the shoulder. It arose as the result of crossings of lhasa apsos with Maltese dogs by breeders in the San Francisco Bay area, beginning in the 1950s. Although long-coated, the length of the hair of kyi leo is shorter than that of its ancestors, and it is regarded as being more robust than the Maltese. It has been developed essentially as a companion dog, and is usually black and white in coloration, although other colour variants crop up occasionally.

The popularity of the kyi leo appears to be spreading further afield, with examples of the breed now living in Canada. Whether it will achieve broader support will probably depend primarily on its exhibition potential. The main reasons for the shar-pei's successful comeback was its strange appearance. With its wrinkled skin and unusual coat texture, it created immediate interest among breeders seeking something different.

With so much emphasis now on the exhibition of pure-bred dogs, rather than their working abilities, if a new breed is to thrive, it will need to do well in the show ring. There is, however, particularly in North America, keen interest in a number of the rarer breeds. In time, assuming their numbers increase sufficiently, these can be moved into the appropriate major breed grouping. A similar system is also used in Britain and elsewhere, to add to the established list of show breeds. Approximately half of the world's 350 breeds are likely to be encountered in Britain.

While exhibiting dogs so they can be judged against an established standard for the breed concerned is a widespread pastime, there are still opportunities for dogs to display their traditional working skills. This applies particularly in the case of gundogs. They can be entered for field trials, as well as participating in the show ring.

Different countries tend to have different systems for classifying breeds. In Britain, the Kennel Club (KC) adopts the following categories: terrier, hound, gundog, working, utility and toy divisions, whereas in the United States, there are non-sporting and sporting groupings, replacing the utility and gundog classes associated with British shows. The rare breeds in the United States are to be found in the aptly named miscellaneous class. Nevertheless, the same breeds are not consistently recognized by both the KC and the American Kennel Club (AKC).

The European authority, known as the Federation Cynologique Internationale

(FCI), operates a more detailed system, comprised of ten distinct groupings, which relate more directly to the breed's original function. There is a division for herding and sheepdogs, and another for coursing dogs, such as the borzoi. In addition, the FCI recognizes a wider range of breeds than either the KC or the AKC, many of which are still localized within a particular area.

Under certain circumstances, these can then attract a much wider audience, particularly today when dog breeding is subject more to the whims of fashion than the production of quality working animals. The pharaoh hound provides such an example. It was probably introduced to the island of Malta by Phoenician seafarers, and it has a very distinctive, prick-eared appearance. Its sleek outline is emphasized by its short, reddish-tan coloration, broken only by a white tip to the tail, and occasionally, a small area of white on the chest.

Up until 1970, the pharaoh hound was virtually unknown outside its native

LEFT: *The Borzoi has excellent sight and is very fast, an ideal combination of attributes for chasing game.*

35

island, where it had evolved over the course of millennia in total isolation. It was used to hunt rabbits and other quarry, and although considered primarily to be a sight hound, it also possesses tracking skills. There is a record of a few of these hounds being brought to Britain in the 1930s, but at that stage, they attracted little interest, and died out. Then, nearly forty years later, further examples were imported; suddenly, breeders were captivated by these hounds, which underwent a massive surge in popularity. They were soon granted championship status by the Kennel Club, and proved equally popular in North America. Here the Canadians were the first to recognize the breed in 1979, and four years later, the American Kennel Club followed suit.

While the pharaoh hound remains one of the most striking examples of how breeds can build up support, there is also a group of dogs which are long-standing international favourites, both in the show ring and the home. They include the labrador retriever and the German shepherd dog (which was known for a period as the Alsatian).

It is interesting to note how such breeds have reached this level of popularity, especially when there are other, similar dogs being bred, which have remained relatively unknown. There is not always an obvious explanation, with the shepherd dogs being a typical example of this phenomenon.

Only the German shepherd dog is well known to the dog-owning public. But there are also the Belgian shepherd dogs, which are descended from similar ancestral stock to the German breed. In this case, there are actually four different varieties, which are sometimes considered as separate breeds themselves. The Groenendael is distinguished by its black coloration, with the Tervuren being of a more variable shade. The Malinois is short-coated, while the Laekenois has a rough, wiry texture to its coat.

A similar situation used to apply in the case of the German shepherd dog, although today, the smooth-coated form is preferred. Occasional long-haired puppies are still produced in some litters, but the wire-haired version of this breed is now exceptionally rare.

The Netherlands is the origin of another, even rarer, member of the northern European shepherd dog group,

FACING PAGE: *Their powerful hind legs make German shepherd dogs great runners and jumpers.*

known as the Hollandse herdershond. Again, there are three distinctive varieties, based on the type of coat, but this breed is even rarer than its Belgian relative. It is still virtually unknown outside its homeland. The smooth-coated Dutch shepherd dog remains most numerous, with both wire- and long-coated forms being particularly hard to find today.

The main reason underlying the dominance of the smooth-coated shepherd dog, as distinct from the international popularity of the German breed, is relatively straightforward to explain. It can be linked to the fact that these dogs are now rarely kept for traditional working purposes. While a rough or long coat gives added protection against the elements, it represents time-consuming grooming for the pet owner. As a result, many people prefer to choose the smooth-coated version of a breed.

A number of other factors also influence the choice of someone seeking a pet dog, and these, in turn, may have an

RIGHT: *Distinctive breeds of pointer are found in Germany (shown here), Spain, Portugal, France, Italy, Belgium, Britain and Denmark.*

overall impact on the numbers of the breed. Although today, interest among exhibitors is important to a breed's development in the first instance, its popularity with the dog-owning public is perhaps more significant in the long term. This is because there needs to be interest in the breed as a companion, to provide an outlet for puppies which will not be suitable, because of minor flaws in their configuration, for the show ring.

Aside from the shepherd dogs, there are a number of other breeds living across Europe which share a common ancestry. Eight individual types of pointer are recognized in France, although the distinguishing characteristics between them may not be very evident in some instances, being essentially local variants.

Pointers as a group were bred from ancestral hound stock, utilizing their scenting skills to indicate the presence of quarry, initially hares, which could then be coursed (caught) by greyhounds with their superior pace. Their name is derived from the way in which they adopt a characteristic frozen stance, pointing in the direction of the quarry.

As shooting became more widespread, so the skills of pointers were sought to reveal the presence of quarry which could then be flushed out, providing a target for the waiting guns. Today, these breeds still tend to be kept primarily by hunters rather than simply as pets, although they form a strong bond with their owners.

The importance of colour

Those seeking a pure-bred dog as a pet often do not delve sufficiently into the breed's background. They tend to concentrate instead largely on its immediate visual appeal. It is not perhaps a coincidence that many owners prefer light-coloured dogs, or those showing prominent areas of white on their coats, simply because this is far removed from the popular image of the grey wolf.

The impact of a change in coloration could also have been linked to a change in temperament. While information on any association between the colour of the coat and behaviour in wolves has not been obtained, it is clear, at least in the case of red foxes, that mutant amber forms are more docile by nature. A similar phenomenon might have been observed in early dogs.

Unfortunately, it is impossible to trace the development of coloration in domestic dogs. Apart from the black-and-white dogs (see page 15), it does appear, from the mummified remains of some discovered in Egypt, that solid-coloured individuals were being bred at an early stage there.

There were also obvious selection pressures for early working dogs to be of a particular colour, in order to carry out their tasks effectively. The maremma sheepdog, whose ancestors were kept by the Romans, is a typical example. These powerful dogs, standing nearly 76 cm(30 in) tall at the shoulder, are pure white in colour. Their original purpose was not primarily to herd sheep; instead, they served to guard flocks from attacks by wolves. Their coloration enabled them to blend in well amongst the sheep, and would also identify them from a distance. A shepherd could therefore be in no doubt as to whether a wolf was in amongst the flock, or his dog.

Similar breeds were developed in other

LEFT: *Visual appeal, particularly coloration, is very significant in most owner's choice of dog.*

parts of Europe and Asia. The kuvasz, from Hungary, is very similar to the maremma sheepdog in appearance. There is also the komandor, which is another flock guardian by tradition, and white in colour. An unusual feature of this particular breed is its coat, which is corded. It is a characteristic shared with another Hungarian breed, called the puli, and may indicate a common ancestry. While the komandor kept a watchful eye on the sheep, protecting them from wolves and other potential predators, the smaller puli served as a herding dog, controlling the movements of the sheep. Neither breed is born with a corded coat; this starts to become apparent when puppies are between six and nine months old, and it can take two years for the cords to develop to their full extent.

The hound group

It is possible to divide today's breeds into six basic categories, in terms of their origins, which in turn influence their behaviour and temperament. These represent perhaps the most natural divisions, without paralleling show classifications exactly.

ABOVE: *Beautiful though they are, Afghan hounds are demanding pets, needing plenty of grooming and exercise.*

41

The close relationship between people and dogs was linked initially to the fact that dogs could assist in hunting, with their pace being superior to that of a human. This led to the development of the hounds. As hunting on horseback became more widespread, so divisions became more evident within this category of dogs. Traditionally, sight hounds such as the greyhound and saluki were used to chase and run down quarry. Possessing keen eyesight and being fleet of foot, they could identify and then pursue a variety of creatures ranging from hares to small antelopes. Later, possibly with game less evident, scent hounds were selectively bred. As their name suggests, they relied predominantly on their tracking skills to locate quarry. Solidly built, these hounds also possessed plenty of stamina. They normally hunted in packs.

It is possible to distinguish between these two types of hound by their appearance. Sight hounds are relatively slender, with a deep chest, giving a good lung capacity to meet their oxygen requirement. They have long, but quite slender legs, and a so-called 'roach' back, which slopes down over the hindquarters to the tail. The most significant feature, how-

FACING PAGE: Salukis are typical sight hounds, having keen eyesight and being fast runners.

ever, is their facial shape. Sight hounds have a long, somewhat triangular-shaped head which narrows towards the nostrils. The eyes are prominently positioned, to give an excellent field of vision. Although some, such as the greyhound and whippet, are smooth-coated, others such as the Afghan hound, have a relatively long coat, which has tended to become more profuse following its entry into the show ring.

There used to be a much greater divergence in the appearance of the Afghan, which was kept over a wide area of Afghanistan and neighbouring countries. Early examples of the breed seen in the West during the 1920s were relatively light in colour, and quite small. Later imports from a more mountainous part of the country were bigger and sturdier, with darker coats, and at first breeders maintained these divisions. The light-coloured Afghans were described as being of the Bell-Murray strain, with their darker relatives establishing the foundations for the Ghasni bloodline, although these divisions have since been lost during the intervening seventy years or so. Although they are highly attractive dogs, Afghan hounds need considerable

Terrier breeds

The terriers are another group of personable dogs, some of which, including the Dandie Dinmont and Bedlington, often attract comment because of their striking appearances. The vast majority of today's terrier breeds arose in Britain, coming to prominence during the last century. Breeds such as the fox terrier were considered vital for the smooth running of hunts, serving to flush foxes out from underground. In the increasing urbanization which resulted from the Industrial Revolution, small dogs were acquired to control the almost inevitable increase in rodents, which found cities and ports well suited to their life-style.

Terriers are highly effective killers of rats and similar vermin. In fact, their abilities were put to the test in Victorian rat pits, with terriers being released into an area with rats, and encouraged to kill as many as possible in the shortest possible space of time. This was a popular form of entertainment in pubs, alongside the early dog shows, well before the karaoke machine!

One of the most famous of all the ratting terriers called 'Billy', managed to kill one hundred rats in just six minutes and thirteen seconds. He was a Manchester terrier, a breed whose origins include whippet blood. This can be seen from the sloping back and the ear shape of this sleek black-and-tan breed.

In the late eighteenth and early nineteenth centuries, when terriers were being selectively bred in Britain, the relative lack of communication meant that breeds were localized. As a result, the terrier breeds of today are generally known under their regional names, reflecting the area of the country where they were first developed.

There is also considerable diversity in their appearance. Slimline breeds such as the Manchester and the Bedlington or Rothbury terrier, bred in the north-east of England, are in noticeable contrast to heavyweight breeds such as the Staffordshire bull terrier, and the short-legged, thick-set members of this group, including the popular West Highland white terrier, often better-known affectionately as the 'Westie'.

Having been bred to work outdoors, many varieties of terrier have coarse, wiry coats, which offer good protection against the elements. Some breeds, such as the

FACING PAGE: *Terrier breeds are often known by their regional names – for example, the West Highland terrier.*

ABOVE: The name 'basset' comes from the French word bas, meaning low, which describes the basset hound's stature.

enabling them to be seen when the rest of their body may be obscured in undergrowth. By nature scent hounds are lively, gregarious dogs, and make good companions, although they may well prove rather wayward at times. They also have a gluttonous streak, and are not above stealing food.

Their short hair means that grooming is straightforward, and the use of a hound brush will impart a good gloss to their coats. The smaller breeds of scent hound arose from the need to have short-legged hounds to accompany hunters on foot, rather than on horseback.

The pack hounds with the shortest legs are the various bassets, of which the basset hound itself is the best known. But there is a much wider range of bassets, some of which, including the basset fauve de Bretagne, have a relatively hard-textured coat. The majority of the basset breeds originated in France.

The well-known dachshund, irreverently called the sausage dog, is even shorter than the various bassets. These German hounds were bred originally to catch rabbits and other quarry in underground burrows. Occurring in smooth, wire-haired and long-haired versions, there are now also miniature forms of the dachshund.

The wire coat of dachshunds and other hounds probably affords some protection against sharp vegetation when they are in undergrowth. Sharp twigs and briars are caught up in the coat rather than penetrating into the skin.

Gundogs

Dogs with similar coats are well represented within the gundog grouping. This division, which traces its origins back to the first spaniels, now embraces a much wider range of breeds, some of which have been bred to operate in very specific terrain. A number of these dogs willingly take to water, and prove good swimmers. Both the labrador and curly-coated retrievers are in this category, as is the poodle.

Probably the most distinctive of all breeds, the case of the poodle reveals how domestication can distort the origins of a working breed. The poodle is of ancient lineage, thought to have been developed in Germany and France about 600 years ago. Its highly manicured appearance today is rooted in its ancestral past, with poodles originally being kept to retrieve ducks in marshland, a task which demanded both stamina and swimming ability.

While its relatively long, dense coat could prove a liability in water, this hair would serve to insulate the body when the poodle plunged into freezing temperatures. A compromise arose whereby the chest area was left protected by hair, as were the joints, while much of the hindquarters were shorn, to assist the dog's swimming abilities. The tip was left on the tail, to aid recognition.

Today, there are three distinct sizes of poodle, of which the standard form is the oldest. The trend towards miniaturization led first to the emergence of the miniature, and then the toy poodle, as the breed's distinctive appearance found favour as a companion in palaces across Europe. Today's toy poodles are about half the size of the standard variety, averaging around 20 cm (8 in) in height at the shoulder. As in other cases, this trend towards a reduction in size has led to a corresponding increase in health problems, ranging from difficulties in giving birth through to weak kneecaps.

Poodles are similar to other gundogs in

LEFT: *Pointers were developed for use in recreational hunting in the nineteenth century.*

terms of their temperament. They work closely with people, and are easy to train. Part of the reason for the rise in their popularity was the fact that they could be taught a variety of tricks, which placed them in front of a wider audience. Poodles have gained a reputation as circus performers through the ages, their dependable natures ensuring that they were unlikely to fail in front of an audience.

Terrier breeds

The terriers are another group of personable dogs, some of which, including the Dandie Dinmont and Bedlington, often attract comment because of their striking appearances. The vast majority of today's terrier breeds arose in Britain, coming to prominence during the last century. Breeds such as the fox terrier were considered vital for the smooth running of hunts, serving to flush foxes out from underground. In the increasing urbanization which resulted from the Industrial Revolution, small dogs were acquired to control the almost inevitable increase in rodents, which found cities and ports well suited to their life-style.

Terriers are highly effective killers of rats and similar vermin. In fact, their abilities were put to the test in Victorian rat pits, with terriers being released into an area with rats, and encouraged to kill as many as possible in the shortest possible space of time. This was a popular form of entertainment in pubs, alongside the early dog shows, well before the karaoke machine!

One of the most famous of all the ratting terriers called 'Billy', managed to kill one hundred rats in just six minutes and thirteen seconds. He was a Manchester terrier, a breed whose origins include whippet blood. This can be seen from the sloping back and the ear shape of this sleek black-and-tan breed.

In the late eighteenth and early nineteenth centuries, when terriers were being selectively bred in Britain, the relative lack of communication meant that breeds were localized. As a result, the terrier breeds of today are generally known under their regional names, reflecting the area of the country where they were first developed.

There is also considerable diversity in their appearance. Slimline breeds such as the Manchester and the Bedlington or Rothbury terrier, bred in the north-east of England, are in noticeable contrast to heavyweight breeds such as the Staffordshire bull terrier, and the short-legged, thick-set members of this group, including the popular West Highland white terrier, often better-known affectionately as the 'Westie'.

Having been bred to work outdoors, many varieties of terrier have coarse, wiry coats, which offer good protection against the elements. Some breeds, such as the

FACING PAGE: *Terrier breeds are often known by their regional names – for example, the West Highland terrier.*

Lakeland terrier, which were developed in the Lake District region of England, still remain relatively localized, whereas others, including the Yorkshire terrier, have become well known internationally. This latter breed has contributed to the development of the Australian silky terrier. Although the Yorkshire terrier may appear rather delicate, with its long trailing coat reaching down the sides of its body to the ground, this breed still retains keen hunting instincts and should not be viewed as a lap dog.

In terms of temperament, terriers tend to be alert and active, and although not especially social with other dogs, they usually develop a strong bond with their owners. The largest member of the group is the Airedale terrier, which stands up to 61 cm (24 in) tall at the shoulder. It is named after the River Aire in southern Yorkshire, where the ancestors of this breed were kept to hunt otters and badgers.

Undoubtedly, the most notorious and feared of the terrier breeds is the American pit bull terrier, which is a relatively recent creation in its present form. Ownership of these aggressive dogs is now outlawed or restricted in a number of

countries. Pit bull terriers are not of recognizable type, however, compared with other breeds.

As a result, owners of other similar terriers, such as Staffordshire bull terriers, have found themselves accused of harbouring unregistered pit bull terriers in cases that have been brought before English courts. Not only can American pit bull terriers be very aggressive towards other dogs, being used in illegal dogfights, but these terriers may also attack people without provocation.

Companion breeds

In marked contrast to the American pit bull terrier, the breeds which have been developed as companion dogs are ideally suited as household pets for families with children. The majority of the dogs in this category are relatively small, although there tends to be far more diversity in appearance than is the case with several other groups, such as hounds. This is

LEFT: *Most of the terrier breeds known today, including the Staffordshire terrier, were developed in Britain.*

because human fashion, rather than any underlying practical function, has been the dominant force in their development. Perhaps not surprisingly therefore, there may be a greater incidence of health problems in these dogs, compared with those in other categories.

One of the most widespread is patellar luxation, when the kneecaps or patellae are not properly supported, and typically move to the inner side of the leg. This gives the dog a bow-legged stance, and in severe cases, it results in difficulty in walking. Surgery may help to stabilize the problem, however, but affected dogs should not be used for breeding purposes, since this condition is likely to be inherited.

A number of the companion dogs have long coats, which require daily grooming in order to maintain their appearance and to prevent the hair from becoming matted. Several smaller versions of larger breeds are typically included in this group as well, such as the toy poodle, and

LEFT: *The Pekingese was designed to be small, cuddly and affectionate.*

some spitz dogs. The latter include most of the German spitz breeds which, like their bigger relatives, are characterized by their small, erect, triangular-shaped ears, and the plumed tail which curls down over the back.

One of the most popular of the companion breeds today is the Cavalier King Charles spaniel, which is actually a newcomer, developed during the 1920s. This breed is the result of a deliberate attempt to re-create the old appearance of the spaniels which were much in evidence at the court of King Charles II. During the 1920s, an American enthusiast called Roswell Eldridge offered substantial cash prizes for spaniels which resembled those which had existed at that stage. They could be distinguished from the King Charles spaniel, as the breed had then become known, by their much longer noses, and slightly larger build.

This provided the stimulus for the re-creation of this older style of spaniel, which has currently eclipsed its modern relative in popularity. The separation between the two breeds was completed in 1944, when the Kennel Club established a separate standard for the type of King Charles spaniel inspired by Eldridge,

adding the prefix of 'Cavalier' to the breed name, in order to separate them.

Many Eastern breeds of ancient lineage are still popular as companion dogs, including the Pekingese, which was a favourite of the ruling dynasties in China for millennia, before being brought to Britain when the Imperial Palace in Peking was overrun in 1860. The small size of the Pekingese meant that they used to be called sleeve dogs, because they could be carried within the flowing sleeves of courtiers.

A close relative of the Pekingese, rather inappropriately called the Tibetan 'spaniel' (although it is not related to the true spaniels), as well as the popular pug, also came from this part of the world, as did the lhasa apso, another old Tibetan breed which has found its way to the West quite recently, during the present century.

Light coloration tends to be a feature of many of the companion dogs. Those of bichon stock may be the oldest, being characterized by their whitish coats and rather long hair. Typical examples in this case are the bichon frise, which used to have a strong following in the royal palaces of Europe, and its relatives, including the Bolognese, a breed which was developed in the southern part of Italy, and the coton de tulear. This latter breed is thought to have evolved from bichons taken by the French to Madagascar, off Africa's east coast, during the sixteenth century.

Working breeds

The sixth and final grouping, comprising general working breeds, encompasses an even more diverse range of dogs. Some are highly specialized, having been bred for a specific purpose over the course of centuries. A typical example is the lundehund, or Norwegian puffin dog. A relatively small dog, averaging about 13 in (33 cm) at the shoulder, its origins date back to the sixteenth century.

Few breeds are more specialized or better equipped for their highly dangerous work. Lundehunds have been used for centuries to scale the cliffs around Norway's coast in search of nesting puffins. They have very well-developed feet, with at least six toes present on each foot, to help them to retain a grip. Entering narrow crevices in the rocks also demands considerable agility, and apart from possessing extra joints in their feet, the lundehund also has a double-jointed neck, which enables it to twist its neck down on to its back. The forelimbs can be turned at almost 90° to the body as well, so it can twist its way into and out of narrow openings with little risk of becoming trapped or falling. At one time on the verge of extinction, the numbers of lundehunds have since increased, and the future of this unique breed appears to be secure.

Many of the northern working breeds are of spitz descent, characterized by their prick ears, and the tail which normally curves to one side of the body. The laikas, with several different forms recognized throughout eastern Europe and Asia, are typical of this group, but they are not well known outside their area of origin. These are multi-purpose dogs, able to pull sleighs and hunt, as well as being alert guardians around property. They also played a part in the early Russian space programme.

In the far north, where the land is under snow for much of the year, it is doubtful if human settlement would have been possible on any scale, without the assistance of dogs. They provided vital transport in an era before machines, which have tended to displace them. Nevertheless, breeds such as the white samoyed and the Siberian husky, as well as the Alaskan malamute from North America, have now become much more widely kept. They still retain a strong pack instinct, and may prove strong-willed on occasions, but these are the very attributes which have led to their survival in the frozen north over the course of centuries.

As within the other breed groupings, certain working dogs have built up a huge international following. These include the Dobermann, a German breed named after a tax collector called Louis Dobermann, who was responsible for the breed's development.

Bred during the last century, the aggressive side of the Dobermann's nature was encouraged at first, since it served to protect its owner against thieves and unwanted harassment. Since then, however, its sleek, sculptured appearance

RIGHT: *With its instinct for herding other animals, the border collie is a natural sheepdog.*

has seen its popularity soar in the show ring, where it was vital to ensure that such dogs were of even temperament, and would not resent the close attention of judges.

The protective nature of some working dogs has been channelled into helping those in need, and the life-saving tradition of the St Bernard is renowned throughout the world. The ancestors of these gentle giants were first kept at the Hospice of St Bernard de Menthon, high in the Swiss Alps, nearly 1,000 years ago. They may be descended from the mastiff breeds of ancient Rome, and have saved lives in the Alps since the early 1700s. One of the most famous of all St Bernards, called Barry, is credited with having rescued forty people, and overall, more than 2,500 people are said to owe their lives to these dogs.

Down the centuries, tragedy has struck on occasions. Barry himself was killed by a petrified traveller, while the kennels

LEFT: *Dobermanns are powerful dogs, requiring firm training from puppyhood to curb their dominant instincts.*

LEFT: *The Bernese mountain dog may not be the ideal pet for everyone, having a large (and costly!) appetite.*

have been struck by avalanches and serious outbreaks of the killer viral disease distemper, which resulted in heavy loss of life, before the advent of vaccinations. The breed is now kept in many countries, but these are not dogs suitable for confined suburban living.

Yet with such a huge diversity of dog breeds now available, often far away from their country of origin, it is quite possible to select a breed which should fit in well to almost any environment. Even so, it is vital that a prospective dog owner should also be prepared to allow sufficient time to care properly for their pet on a daily basis, and exercise it, bearing in mind that this is a commitment which will need to last for a decade or more.

CHAPTER FOUR

Dogs as Companions

In our society today, dogs are kept mainly as companions, although some are used for traditional working purposes as well. They have also been trained successfully to undertake new tasks, with guide dogs providing a fine example of how dogs can make life easier for people suffering from impaired vision. A more recent innovation has been the use of dogs to alert those afflicted by poor hearing to sounds in their environment, such as a ringing doorbell, of which they may otherwise be unaware.

Dogs are also present behind the scenes at airports and ports, alerting the authorities to any concealed drugs or explosives in luggage or freight. Various breeds, ranging from spaniels to retrievers have proved able to carry out these tasks to such a high degree of accuracy that their lives have actually been threatened by criminals.

Even for the average pet dog, however, life has changed immeasurably since the turn of the century. The prepared dog food market has expanded dramatically, and, as a result of this commercial pressure, there has been a massive amount of expenditure on research to unravel the dog's nutritional requirements. The dog owner of today is faced with a bewildering array of brands of food for their pet. Not only is there canned food, but also semi-moist as well as dried diets which compete for shelf space in pet shops and supermarkets.

The convenience factor, when it comes to feeding a dog, has helped to ensure

FACING PAGE: *Regular dog-walking will help to raise your own overall level of fitness, as well as being good for your dog.*

59

their continued popularity. There is no need to worry about buying and cooking a range of meats for a dog, and ensuring that it is receiving a balanced diet. Everything can be acquired, ready for use, in a packet or can. Throughout the European Union, there are currently estimated to be around 27 million dogs in total, with a similar number being kept in North America. Britain's dog population has now risen to 7 million.

As research continues, so manufacturers are seeking new niche markets, with canine life-style diets growing in popularity. Different diets for puppies, active dogs, middle-aged dogs and old dogs are assuming greater prominence on the shelves. But this does not necessarily mean that dogs are healthier today than they were in days gone by. Obesity afflicts approximately a third of all dogs, and this is not merely the result of overfeeding with the apparently endless supply of treats now available. Dogs are simply not having sufficient exercise.

They are driven around in cars, let out for a brief run in the park, and then taken home to resume their sedentary life. A growing incidence of heart disease and other complications linked to obesity,

ABOVE: *A dog's sense of smell is highly developed; here, a police dog undergoes training to detect explosives by scent.*

FACING PAGE: *To stay healthy, dogs require more than an occasional brief run in the park.*

few owners cut back on the amount of food that they provide.

Constant striving for success in the show ring can on occasions also prove detrimental to the overall health of a particular breed. The fashion for producing bulldogs with larger heads and flatter faces than their Victorian counterparts has meant that an increasing number of puppies have to be born by Caesarean section, as their heads are simply too big to pass normally through their mother's birth canal. Subsequently the flattened face gives them less opportunity to cool down, and they are then more susceptible to heat stroke. Changes in show standards and the attitudes of judges are now helping to overcome such problems however, which gives hope for the future in this case.

Screening programmes have also been instituted for other hereditary ailments, such as progressive retinal atrophy (PRA), which leads to an irreversible loss of vision. This is the result of degenerative changes in the dog's retina at the back of the eye, from where the image is transmitted to the brain.

Another condition of particular concern is hip dysplasia (HD), particularly in

such as *diabetes mellitus*, is starting to emerge, and may increase in the future, unless the average pet dog's life-style alters significantly.

The trend towards responsible ownership – neutering pets so that they will not produce unwanted puppies – is potentially worsening the situation. This is because neutering reduces the dog's nutritional requirements markedly, but

the larger breeds. Affected individuals show signs of lameness, and the hip joints are painful, with the symptoms tending to become progressively worse.

When contemplating the purchase of puppies which may be at risk of developing either problem, it is important to check that their parents were properly screened. Although this will not provide an absolute guarantee that the puppy will not be afflicted, the risk should be considerably lessened.

When it comes to choosing a puppy of a particular breed, it is important to appreciate that more ordinary pure-bred puppies are available than those which are likely to excel in the show ring.

Should you require a puppy which is likely to do well in the show ring, then you must be willing to pay correspondingly more. This does not guarantee you success of course: such puppies simply

LEFT: *If you are simply looking for a pet, it will not matter if a puppy is not of show standard, providing it is healthy.*

FACING PAGE: *Many dog seekers are keen to start out with a puppy, so that it will grow up with their children.*

display better conformation, approximating more closely to the show standard in the breeder's judgement.

There is no standard price for pedigree puppies. A number of other factors, aside from show potential, will influence the asking price. The prestige of the bloodline, for example, is an important factor, with leading breeders tending to charge more for all their puppies.

There is a belief that mongrels are healthier than pedigree dogs. While it is certainly true that they are not at such risk from inherited weaknesses, they are just as susceptible to the major viral illnesses and other conditions which dogs may suffer from during their lives.

When starting out with a mongrel puppy, you are also faced with uncertainty as to its likely adult size. With a pure-bred dog, however, reference to the breed standard will indicate its future growth potential. In the case of a mongrel look at its feet; if these appear relatively large, then it is likely to grow up into a large dog.

Puppies are independent by about nine weeks old, and ready to go to a new home at this stage. They should be bright-eyed and active although they will tend to sleep for longer periods than older dogs.

It is always a good idea to arrange a veterinary check-up for a new puppy as soon as possible, to ensure that it is in the best of health. This also provides an opportunity to discuss vaccinations and deworming. In the past, many dogs died prematurely from killer viral illnesses such as distemper.

Today, however, the risk from these diseases is minimal, with protective vaccines widely available. They are most unlikely to have any adverse effect on the dog, and protection against a number of such diseases can be given in a single shot.

The types of illness now affecting dogs tend to be more the diseases of old age. Tumours of various types and chronic kidney failure are relatively common. But advances in surgical techniques and anaesthesia mean that such conditions which necessitate an operation can be carried out with increasing certainty that the dog will subsequently recover and have a reasonable quality of life afterwards.

With the increasing volume of traffic today, the number of dogs being killed or injured on the roads is growing alarmingly. Puppies are especially vulnerable, as they will run off readily if the opportunity presents itself, before they are properly trained. Skilled orthopaedic surgery may be needed in such cases, and most modern veterinary practices have facilities for taking radiographs of suspected fractures by means of X-rays.

Some people believe that the stresses of modern living affect not only owners, but also dogs themselves. There is no denying the fact that canine behavioural problems have certainly become the focus of greater attention in recent years, partly as a result of media coverage of attacks on people by dogs.

Behaviour and training counsellors are now well established, and their expertise can help to overcome problems which the dog owner is unable to resolve in home surroundings. This in turn can enable people to enrich their lives with the pleasure of owning a well-behaved dog.

RIGHT: *If you want to buy a puppy as a companion, consider a cross-breed rather than a more expensive pedigree dog.*

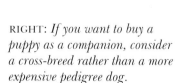

It's a Dog's Life

At birth, after a gestation period lasting approximately 63 days, puppies are totally dependent on their mother.

They will start to suckle soon after being born, and this so-called first milk or colostrum is vital to their subsequent well-being. It contains protective antibodies, which help to guard them against infection until their own immune systems are fully functional.

For the first two weeks of their lives, the puppies will not be able to hear or see, and they will be unable to wag their tails. The bitch will stay with them almost constantly, and if a puppy becomes displaced, it will drag itself blindly around until it locates her.

The mother will even stimulate them to relieve themselves, by licking their coats.

Most of their time is spent sleeping.

Changes become noticeable from the age of about three weeks. The puppies' eyes open, and they start to respond to sounds in their environment. The bitch's milk is rich in fats and proteins, and ensures they develop rapidly. The puppies start to move around more, and by a month old they are likely to be showing an interest in solid food. Their first set of teeth begins to emerge from the gums at this stage, and these will be retained for the first six months of life, until they are replaced by a permanent set.

The bitch will start to spend less time with her litter, and is likely to resent their attempts to suckle, especially as their emerging sharp teeth are liable to hurt her. They will then switch increasingly to

ABOVE: *A litter of nine-day-old border collie puppies curl up together for a nap.*

a diet of solids as her milk supply dries up.

In order to meet their requirements as they grow, approximately twice as much food as normal will be needed by the puppies. This is given in three or four portions through the day. Gradually, the number of meals should be cut back, to perhaps just a single daily feed, with a correspondingly larger quantity of food, by the time they are adult.

The puppyhood phase is generally assumed to have passed once the young dog is six months old, but studies suggest that there is a key socialization period, relatively early in the dog's life, typically extending from about four to twelve weeks after birth. A puppy which has been kept in relative isolation from people throughout this stage will tend to be nervous and withdrawn for the remainder of its life. This is why it is usually recommended to transfer the puppy to its new home by about nine weeks old, so it can adjust to its new surroundings. Here it will be able to explore and settle down, although it is inadvisable to allow the young puppy out into public places until the initial course of vaccinations is complete, at twelve weeks of age.

Domestic breeds of dog show many of the characteristics of their wild relatives. Scent plays an important part in their social interactions, with urine in particular being used for scent-marking purposes. Unlike wild canids, however, dogs have acquired a further means of communication with each other and their owners, by barking.

This trait has presumably been encouraged, as the dog has been persuaded to adopt a protective role in human society. Although grey wolves do bark, this is a much quieter, less conspicuous vocalization, which is typically uttered as a warning call close to the pack's den. It does not have a threatening quality, unlike barking. Instead, when it comes to maintaining territorial boundaries from incursions by neighbouring packs, wolves will howl loudly, with such calls echoing over a wide area.

While wild canids generally have long limbs relative to their body size, which enables them to move quite rapidly, this characteristic is less evident with domestication. It is most apparent in hound breeds however, which are built for pace. The movement, or 'gait', of the different breeds may differ markedly, and this is often featured in the show standard. As a result, judges expect to see the dogs before them trotting and running around the ring with their owners for a period, before arriving at any decisions on the placings in a class.

The reasonably rigid structure of the dog's limbs provides support when the dog is running, but it precludes effective climbing. Maintaining balance is important when running at speed, and the dog's horny pads help to provide support. But in spite of their hard appearance, they will bleed profusely if sliced on a piece of broken glass, and will probably have to be bound up under these circumstances, to reduce haemorrhaging until the dog can receive veterinary attention.

The nails also offer support, especially on wet ground. They are not thin and curved, like those of a cat, but relatively broad and blunt at their tips. On occasions, nails can become overgrown, and will have to be trimmed back carefully, to prevent any risk of bleeding.

RIGHT: *Barking has been encouraged as a canine trait, as dogs have been developed to take a protective role.*

69

Dogs show a reduction in the number of digits in contact with the ground, with their innermost digits on each foot being positioned at a slightly higher point on the side of the legs. These particular claws are described as dew claws, possibly because they would become dampened by dew as the dog walked over a grassy surface.

In a few cases, notably the lundehund, the dew claws provide additional support as the dog moves over rocky and uneven surfaces. But the exposed position of these claws also means that they can easily become snagged in undergrowth, and are liable to be torn.

Since they are not in contact with the ground, there is little if any wear on the claws themselves. These are then likely to become overgrown, and may actually curl round and penetrate into the supporting fleshy pad, causing the dog considerable pain. For these reasons, it is usual for dew claws to be removed while the dog is still a puppy. This is a comparatively minor and painless procedure at this stage, but will require more radical surgery in older dogs. In a few cases however, notably the briard, a herding breed of French origin, there may actually be double dew claws

on each of the hind legs, and these, as a recognized breed characteristic, are not removed in the case of exhibition stock. Instead, the claws must be trimmed back as necessary.

Surgery has also been used more controversially to alter the appearance of various breeds in other ways. Tail docking is usually carried out when puppies are a few days old, and is a practice traditionally linked with terriers in particular. The actual position where the cut is made depends on the breed concerned. Docking was originally carried out to prevent tails being injured when the dogs were working, and has since been incorporated into a number of breed standards. It has become a controversial practice in recent years however, and may ultimately be outlawed.

In Britain, ear cropping has been banned by the Kennel Club for more than a century, but it still flourishes elsewhere in Europe and North America. It entails cutting part of the cartilage of the ear, causing the restructured ear to become erect, although reduced in size. Cropping dramatically alters the appearance of the dog, giving it a more ferocious image. Not surprisingly, this is

RIGHT: *A kelpie dog, working sheep in Australia. Normally, a dog's nails will be worn down as the dog walks and runs over a variety of surfaces.*

therefore usually carried out on larger breeds kept as guardians, such as the Dobermann and Great Dane.

In many cases, dogs have naturally erect ears, and these probably help to capture sound waves effectively. They can be moved slightly, so as to pinpoint the direction of the sound, as shown by the various spitz breeds, which tend to prefer open terrain. While keen hearing would be of value to hounds, raised ears could be positively disadvantageous when they were pursuing quarry through undergrowth. There would be a real risk that the sensitive ear canal could be injured by twigs or thorns in the vegetation. It is for this reason that their ear flaps hang down, protecting the sensitive inner part of the ear.

Aggressive breeds would be disadvan-

71

taged by such large ears however, especially those bred for dogfighting purposes. The ear flaps would provide an easy target for an opponent to seize and shred with strong teeth. Small ears, often set well back on the head, are therefore characteristic of many breeds of terrier.

As dogs are increasingly kept solely as companions, or for show purposes, so aggression is no longer considered desirable, even in breeds originally developed with this characteristic, such as the bull terrier. Dogs must integrate well not only with their owners, but also with their fellow dogs, as when out walking, for example.

The overall level of aggression in dogs has therefore been significantly reduced over the past century. But dogs also have their own body language, entailing a series of ritual movements, before any aggression is likely to be displayed under normal circumstances. Pain or the presence of puppies may result in a more immediate threat of physical attack, however, which will be pressed home until the weaker individual retreats, pursued for a short distance by the dominant dog.

Two dogs meeting for the first time when out for a walk will approach each other warily, sniffing at each other's hindquarters. They may then part, encouraged by their owners, without further contact. If running off the leash, a young dog might bow down on its front legs, then stand up suddenly and bark when it meets another. This should not be misinterpreted as a gesture of aggression, however; it is encouragement to the other dog to play.

But when a dog's territory is threatened, by the incursion of another, then fighting may well be the result. In the home, this may follow the introduction of another dog alongside an established individual. The newcomer is likely to be lavished with attention, and this serves to undermine the dominance order, as the other dog's social status is reduced accordingly. The key to avoiding this sort of encounter is to praise the established dog when introducing a newcomer, reinforcing its position, rather than undermining it. Aggression is also less likely between neutered individuals.

It is not uncommon for male dogs to fight each other when they are pursuing a bitch on heat, who is receptive to mating. Bitches will have regular periods of heat, usually twice a year, throughout

FACING PAGE: *Two young dogs meeting for the first time rarely act aggressively; usually, they will playfully chase each other.*

their lives, and will attract suitors. As a consequence, many owners prefer to have their bitches neutered, to prevent the problems which can arise. Similarly, in the case of male dogs, neutering may be advisable, to decrease aggression, and curb any tendency to stray.

Signs of old age

There may be few evident signs of ageing in some dogs, although in many cases, they become less active. Bad breath is frequently encountered, and may be related to dental problems and gum disease, or to progressive kidney failure.

Changes in coat pigmentation can also accompany the ageing process, particularly in dark-coloured dogs, such as black labrador retrievers. In this instance, the hair around the muzzle will turn grey and then white.

Most dogs today, living as pets, have a life expectancy of at least a decade, with smaller breeds often living well into their teens. There appears not to be a significant difference between the life spans of individual breeds however, aside from the fact that small dogs live longer on average than larger ones.

CHAPTER SIX

Wild Relatives

Members of the family Canidae include foxes, wolves and wild dogs such as coyotes and jackals, not overlooking the African wild dog (*Lycaon pictus*) itself. Wild canids are to be found on every inhabited continent, although Australia is something of an exception. Here, however, the dingo (*Canis dingo*), a feral dog, was brought by the early settlers from Asia perhaps 4,000 years ago, and is now

LEFT: *Most wild canids, such as coyotes, are very adaptable, hunting or scavenging as circumstance permits.*

FACING PAGE: *Wolves have suffered heavily at the hands of humans; in this century, eight sub-species have been wiped out.*

75

widespread, although it is not a native to this country.

In total, there are 34 different species of wild canid surviving on the planet today, and certainly when compared with other mammalian groups, their numbers have not decreased significantly over the past 400 years, since European exploration of the rest of the globe began in earnest. Only one species, the Falkland Island wolf (*Dusicyon australis*), has become extinct during this period, as the direct result of human persecution.

But during the present century, at least eight sub-species of the grey wolf have been eliminated. It used to be one of the most widely distributed of all the larger mammals. Today, only in the far north of the American continent, and in parts of Asia, does it remain numerous.

Its near relative, the red wolf (*Canis rufus*), is effectively extinct in the wild. The continued existence of this species is due entirely to a captive-bred project set up in the 1970s, with a tiny number of survivors. Although a release scheme has begun, its future remains precarious.

But as these larger species, which associate in packs and need relatively big hunting areas, have been subjected to human pressures, so more opportunistic members of the family, such as the coyote (*Canis latrans*) in North America, and the red fox (*Vulpes vulpes*), which also occurs in Europe have exploited the resulting niche. They will hunt or scavenge, eating both animal and plant foods. In the far north, the Arctic fox (*Alopex lagopus*) manages to survive in some of the most inhospitable terrain on earth, eating almost anything it can find.

Similar pressures that have affected the grey wolf have also taken a toll on the African wild dog, which used to roam the plains of Africa in large packs. Fears are now being expressed about the survival of this highly social canid, with its emphasis on the matriarch of the pack. In its social structure, a dominant female is supported by males.

The advantages of social living extend beyond the capture of prey. Helpers are well recognized within jackal populations. These are young animals, which have not yet broken away to form their own territories. Instead, they remain for a year to assist a breeding pair in the rearing of their offspring. They can alert the young jackals to impending danger, and keep them together while the adults are hunt-

FACING PAGE: *The range of the grey wolf has contracted dramatically; it was once found throughout the entire northern hemisphere.*

ABOVE LEFT AND RIGHT: *From their wild ancestry, domestic dogs retain agility, strength and the capacity to adapt to different terrains.*

ing. Yet perhaps surprisingly, much still remains to be learnt about wild canids. In particular, the smaller foxes of both Asia and South America are not well studied, and relatively little is known about their populations.

Some, such as the unusual bush dog (*Speothos venaticus*), appear to be declining, but the reasons in this case are not very clear. A number of other wild canids in South America, notably the grey zorro (*Dusicyon griseus*), which is a form of fox, have been heavily hunted for their fur.

The demand for furs has also underlain the introduction of the racoon dog (*Nyctereutes procyonoides*) to eastern Europe. This Asiatic species is now well established in the wild in Europe. Its name comes from its facial appearance, which is more suggestive of a racoon than a canid. The adaptability of this species provides further evidence that canids can adapt well, as long as hunting pressures on them are not severe. This provides hope for their continued long-term survival in a rapidly changing world.

Index